30 Days of Sex Talks
Empowering Your Child with Knowledge of Sexual Intimacy
Ages 3-7

Rising Parent Media, LLC
© 2015 by Rising Parent Media
Printed in the United States of America

20 19 18 17 16   2 3 4 5

ISBN: 978-0-9863708-0-9 (paperback)

The paper used in this publication meets the minimum require-
ments of the American National Standard for Information Sci-
ences—Permanence of Paper for Printed Library Materials, ANSI
Z39.48-1992.

www.educateempowerkids.org

30 DAYS OF SEX TALKS

EMPOWERING YOUR CHILD WITH KNOWLEDGE OF SEXUAL INTIMACY

BY
EDUCATE AND EMPOWER KIDS

FOR GREAT RESOURCES AND INFORMATION, FOLLOW US:

Facebook: www.facebook.com/educateempowerkids/
Twitter: @EduEmpowerKids
Pinterest: pinterest.com/educateempower/
Instagram: Eduempowerkids

EDUCATE AND EMPOWER KIDS WOULD LIKE TO ACKNOWLEDGE
THE FOLLOWING PEOPLE WHO CONTRIBUTED TIME, TALENTS,
AND ENERGY TO THIS PUBLICATION:

Dina Alexander, MS
Amanda Scott
Jenny Webb, MA
Caron C. Andrews

Ed Allison
Mary Ann Benson, MSW, LSW
Scott Hounsell
Cliff Park, MBA

DESIGN AND ILLUSTRATION BY:
Jera Mehrdad

30 DAYS OF SEX TALKS
TABLE OF CONTENTS

INTRODUCTION

Sexual intimacy is one of the greatest experiences available to us as human beings. We feel that it is imperative that you are able to clearly express this sentiment to your child. Each of us at Educate and Empower Kids is a parent and like all parents, we feel charged with providing positive, thought-provoking experiences for our children to learn from. In the world we live in, this is not an easy task. Our goal is not only to provide you with an opportunity to start conversations about crucial topics, but also to help you create an environment in your home which encourages open discussions about the many other issues which will inevitably come up as you are raising your child. Talking with your child about sex and intimacy is a great way to open the door for other important discussions. After all, this is what makes us human—it's part of what makes the human experience beautiful.

The purpose of this curriculum is to help you as parents establish and grow open and honest communication with your child about sex, intimacy, the dangers of online pornography and your child's view of him or herself. We believe that once you have started these conversations, you will be empowered to talk to your child about anything.

Our mission is to empower families to create deep, meaningful connection. Children in the US spend an average of 7.5 hours consuming media each day (Boyse, RN, 2010). Additionally, according to one study, 42% of children had been exposed to pornography in the past year and of those, 67% were exposed to it accidentally (Wolack, et al., 2007). With the amount of sex and violence in almost every medium our kids are watching, we need to ask ourselves what we are doing to counteract all that screen time.

With this program, we've made it simple for you to talk about the beauty of love, sex, bodies and relationships. You can discuss sex in the context in which it belongs; as a part of a healthy relationship that also includes joy, laughter and the full range of emotion that defines human intimacy.

It's imperative that you begin your daily talks with just one topic in mind and that you make every experience, however brief, truly meaningful.

GETTINGSTARTED

The curriculum includes a book, glossary and topic cards. Each topic is followed by several bullet points. These bullet points contain terms to define and discuss with your child as well as questions or statements designed to inspire conversations between you and your child. We've included definitions, sample dialogue and even some activities to make it simple and to help you get started. If you feel like your child isn't ready to discuss the bullets listed under the topic or if you feel that your child's knowledge is more advanced, please note that we have also developed this curriculum for other age groups and it is available for purchase. It's important to discuss things with your child based on his or her own maturity level; progressing or referring back at your own pace.

The hard work has all been done for you, you need not be an expert. In fact, we feel strongly that leaning on your own personal experiences—both mistakes and successes—is a great way to use life lessons to teach your child. If done properly, these talks will bring you closer to your child than you ever could have imagined. You know and love your child more than anyone, so you decide when and where these discussions take place. In time, you will recognize and enjoy teaching moments in everyday life with your child.

Early in the research for this curriculum, our Vice President had an experience while shopping with her children. As she passed a mall lingerie store with her two young sons, she decided to seize the moment and explain to her boys about body image, photo manipulation and unrealistic portrayals of people in advertising. Soon, you too will recognize and take advantage of moments like these in your own life and your child will be better informed and more prepared because of them. Because the truth is that your child will be exposed to hyper-sexualized media eventually, you need to give him or her the framework to be ready and convey to your child what healthy sexuality really is.

This book works well with the downloadable topic cards (online code is available in the back of the book). On the following pages you'll find each topic with its bullet points listed followed by ideas for further discussion items, questions you may want to ask, and points to consider when talking with your child about that topic. Throughout the book we've also included several suggested scenarios that you could pose to your child to prompt additional thoughts and discussions of specific situations that could arise in his or her life.

As you work through the topics, think about sharing your ideas and your personal or family standards; encouraging your child to share their thoughts and feelings. Talk about both the emotional and physical aspects of each topic and discuss emotional and physical safety. Be sure to ask your child questions to help draw him or her out. These topics are starting points. If additional or different conversations arise, follow them. This curriculum is designed to be personalized by you and your child. Consistent conversation is the key to successfully implementing this program.

Remember, the goal is not only to present useful information to your child, but to normalize the process of talking to each other about these topics.

We strongly encourage you to read through the suggested topics, bullet points, and ideas in the parent book before talking with your child. Here are a few tips:

- Plan ahead of time but don't create an event. Having a plan or planning ahead of time will remove much of the awkwardness you might feel in talking about these subjects with your child. In not creating an event, you are making the discussions feel more spontaneous, the experience more repeatable and yourself more approachable.

- Consider your individual child's age, developmental stage, and personality in conjunction with each topic, as well as your family's values and individual situation, and adapt the material in order to produce the best discussion.

There are additional resources listed in the back of the book as well as a glossary to help you define the terms used.

INSTRUCTIONS

BETHESOURCE

You direct the conversations. Bring up issues that you feel are most important and allow the conversation to flow from there. You love and know your child better than anyone else, so you are the best person to judge what will be most effective: Taking into account personal values, religious beliefs, individual personalities, and family dynamics. Our goal is to provide you with a simple structure and guide for how to introduce and discuss a variety of topics. We want to help you, the parent, be the best source of information about sex and intimacy for your child. If you don't discuss these topics, your child will look for answers from other, less reliable *and sometimes dangerous* sources like: the internet, the media, and other kids.

FOCUSONINTIMACY

Help your child understand how incredible and uniting sex can be. Don't just focus on the mechanics, spend a significant amount of time talking about the beauty of love and sex, the reality of real relationships and how they are built and maintained. Children are constantly exposed to unhealthy examples of relationships in the media. Many of them are teaching your child lessons about sexuality and interactions between people that are misleading, incomplete, and unhealthy. Real emotional intimacy is rarely portrayed, so it's your job to model positive behavior. You can help your child connect the dots between healthy relationships and healthy sexuality when you model positive ways for your child to like and care for his or her body; to protect, have a positive attitude toward and make favorable choices for that body.

ANSWERYOURCHILD'SQUESTIONS

If you are embarrassed by your child's curiosity and questions, you imply that there is something shameful about these topics. However, if you answer your child's questions openly and honestly, you demonstrate that sexuality is positive and healthy relationships are something to seek when the time is right. Answer your child's questions honestly and openly and your child will learn that you are available not just for this discussion, but for any discussion. It's okay if you don't have all the answers. Tell your child you will find out for him or her; because it's better that you go searching instead of your child doing so. See the resources at the end of this book and on our resources page at www.educateempowerkids.org for further information on these and other topics.

BEPOSITIVE

Take the fear and shame out of these discussions. Sex is natural and wondrous and your child should feel nothing but positivity about it from you. If you do feel awkward, try to conceal it with matter-of-fact tones and discussion. It's easier than you think- just open your mouth and begin! *It will get easier with every talk you have with your child.* After a couple of talks, he or she will begin to look forward to this time that you are spending together and so will you. Taking the time to talk about these things will reiterate to your child how important he or she is to you. Use experiences from your own life to begin a discussion if it makes you feel more comfortable. We have listed some tough topics here, but they are all discussed in a positive, informative way. Don't worry, we are with you every step of the way!

NEEDTOKNOW

- This curriculum is not a one-size-fits all. *You* guide the conversation and lead the discussion according to your unique situation.

- No program can cover all aspects of sexual intimacy perfectly for every individual circumstance. You can empower yourself with the knowledge you gain from this program to share with your child what you feel is the most important.

- This program is meant to be simple! It's presented on cards with bullet points to be straightfoward and create conversations.

FINALLY

This program is meant to inspire conversations that we hope assist you in fostering an environment where difficult discussions are made easier. The hope is that your child will feel like he or she can talk to you about anything. This program is a great tool that your kids will look forward to! Take advantage of the one on one time that these discussions facilitate to become more comfortable talking with your child.

It's recommended that you designate with your child and within your home a "safe zone", meaning that during the course of these conversations, your child should feel free and safe to ask any questions and make any comments without judgment or repercussion. Your child should be able to use the term "safe zone" again and again to discuss, confide and consult with you about the tough subjects he or she will be confronted with throughout life.

It's highly recommended that, whenever possible, all parenting parties be involved in these discussions.

Citations

Boyse, RN, K. (2010, August 1). Television (TV) and Children. Retrieved November 13, 2014, from http://www.med.umich.edu/yourchild/topics/tv.htm

Wolack, et al. (2007, February 2). Unwanted and Wanted Exposure to Online Pornography in a National Sample of Youth Internet Users. Retrieved November 13, 2014, from http://pediatrics.aappublications.org/content/119/2/247.full

LET'S GET STARTED!

AGES
3-7

Young children are naturally curious about their bodies and the world around them. This curriculum has been tailored to foster this curiosity by bringing up points that lead towards open and honest conversations that facilitate healthy ways to develop a relationship with one's body. By discussing matters relating to anatomy, relationships, gender, pornography, etc., you will build relationships with open, caring, non-judgmental communication from an early age.

1.
AMAZING BODIES

- ★ WHAT CAN YOUR BODY DO?

- ★ WHY ARE OUR BODIES SPECIAL?

- ★ WHO DOES YOUR BODY BELONG TO?

START THE CONVERSATION

You may wish to direct this conversation to help children see all of the things their bodies can do. Bodies can run, jump, eat, feel, hug, swim, laugh, cry, etc. Emphasize that their bodies are unique, and that they belong to them. Help your child to understand that they experience the world through their body.

SAMPLE ACTIVITY

Have your child touch a book, an ice cube, and their favorite stuffed animal. Prompt them to describe what they feel (hard, soft, hot, cold, etc.). Ask them how they would touch things if they didn't have their hands or skin to feel with. Help them realize that their body informs them about the world that surrounds them.

2.
MY BODY BELONGS TO ME

- ♛ WHY DOES YOUR BODY BELONG TO YOU?

- 💬 I CAN SHARE MY TOYS, BUT I WILL NOT SHARE MY BODY

- ♛ WHAT DOES THE WORD BOUNDARY MEAN?

FORCED AFFECTION: *Pressuring or forcing a child to give a hug, kiss or other form of physical affection when he does not have the desire or inkling to do so.*

START THE CONVERSATION

Explain to your child that because they are unique and special, they are valuable. Help them understand that we take care of things that we value (for example, how do they treat a favorite toy or another special item in your home?). Explain that other people may not understand or respect the child's value and that they need to stand up for themselves. An additional topic that may be covered here is that of forced affection: how do you handle it in your family when someone, such as an aunt, demands a kiss and a hug from your child?

ADDITIONAL QUESTIONS TO CONSIDER

What gives you value?

What makes you special?

What should you do if someone wants to give you a hug and you don't want to?

3.
MALE
ANATOMY

- 💬 PENIS

- 💬 TESTICLE/SCROTUM

- 💬 ANUS

- 👑 WHAT MAKES A BOY DIFFERENT FROM A GIRL?

START THE CONVERSATION

Help your child to understand that these are body parts that boys have. Children may have questions concerning the way a penis can change during an erection. It is completely normal for infants, toddlers, and boys to experience erections for a variety of reasons. They also may have questions regarding what a penis is "for" (at this age, primarily urination). If your child has questions, answer them clearly and avoid associating shame or embarrassment with this natural bodily function. If appropriate, help them understand that a penis is personal and private. If appropriate, help them understand that in the future, the function of the penis goes beyond urination. See glossary for definitions of penis, tesicle/scrotum, and anus.

4.
FEMALE ANATOMY

- VAGINA

- URETHRA

- ANUS

- NIPPLES/BREAST

- WHAT MAKES A GIRL DIFFERENT FROM A BOY?

START THE CONVERSATION

Help your child to understand that these are body parts that girls have. If the child has questions about these body parts, answer the question simply, define terminology, and do not get distracted by additional unnecessary details such as the mechanics of intercourse or birth. See glossary for definitions of vagina, urethra, anus, and nipples/breast..

START THE CONVERSATION

Ask your child what it means for someone to have value.
As you discuss the concept of boundaries, explain that some
people enjoy lots of physical contact, while for other people it
can be uncomfortable and overwhelming. Let your child know
that they can ask people about their boundaries. The goal
during this discussion is to empower your child so that they
know they can ask about other's boundaries.

ADDITIONAL QUESTIONS TO CONSIDER

How would you ask an adult about their boundaries?
Is it ever appropriate to ask adults about their boundaries?
How would you ask a friend about his/her boundaries?
When should you ask friends about their boundaries?

SAMPLE DIALOGUE
(for child to practice)

Can I give you a hug?

Can I hold your hand to cross the street?

5.
RESPECTING OTHERS

- EVERYONE HAS VALUE

- EVERYONE HAS BOUNDARIES

- THESE BOUNDARIES ARE DIFFERENT FOR EACH PERSON

- EVEN IF YOU DON'T LIKE SOMEONE'S BOUNDARIES, YOU STILL RESPECT THEM

6.
PUBLIC

- 👑 WHAT DOES THE WORD "PUBLIC" MEAN?

- 👑 WHAT ARE SOME THINGS WE DO IN PUBLIC?

- 👑 WHAT ARE SOME THINGS WE DO NOT DO IN PUBLIC?

START THE CONVERSATION

It is important for your child to understand the difference between public and private. These can be difficult
concepts for young children, as they rely on an abstract social understanding. To help your child grasp the concept, link "public" with concrete locations and specific behaviors.
As an example, we have provided a sample dialogue to illustrate how this can be done.

SAMPLE DIALOGUE

Parent: "Public" means something that everyone can do, a place where everyone can be, or something that everyone can see.

We are in public when we go to the library, the park, or to school. When we are in public, we can talk, laugh, play, read, eat, walk, etc.

We do not remove our clothing in public. We do not urinate in public. We do not touch our bodies where our underwear covers in public.

Note: Parents, please make sure your child is physically and mentally capable of understanding these rules before they are implemented.

START THE CONVERSATION

It is important for your child to understand the difference between public and private. These can be difficult concepts for young children, as they rely on an abstract social understanding. To help your child grasp the concept, link "private" with concrete locations and specific behaviors. As an example, we have provided a sample dialogue to illustrate how this can be done.

SAMPLE DIALOGUE

Parent: "Private" means something that is just for you, or just for you and your family. We can take baths in private. We go to the bathroom in private. We can be naked in private. Our bedrooms can be private. Our bathrooms can be private.

Developmental Note:
In order to develop a healthy attitude towards privacy and self-sufficiency, it is important to help children understand that they need to go to the bathroom by themselves as soon as they are physically capable of doing so. This does not mean that parents should rush their child to be toilet trained, but rather that after a child is toilet trained (at the point they are ready for it) that they should be encouraged to use the bathroom without their friends or others present. An exception should be made for those who need physical assistance to successfully use a bathroom.

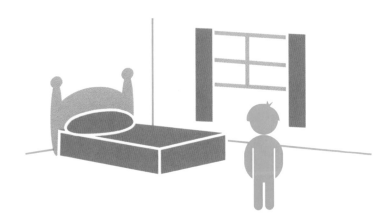

7.
PRIVATE

- ♛ WHAT DOES THE WORD "PRIVATE" MEAN?

- ♛ WHAT ARE SOME THINGS WE DO IN PRIVATE?

- ♛ WHERE ARE PRIVATE PLACES WE GO?

8.
CLOTHING

- WHAT DO WE WEAR TO THE BEACH?

- WHAT DO WE WEAR IN WINTER?

- ONE WAY WE RESPECT AND PROTECT OUR BODIES IS TO WEAR APPROPRIATE CLOTHING

START THE CONVERSATION

Help your child understand the term "appropriate" in terms of an item fitting or working with a specific context. For example, we wear swimsuits at the beach so we can get wet. It would not be appropriate to wear a swimsuit in the middle of a winter snowstorm because we would get cold and possibly sick.

ADDITIONAL QUESTIONS TO CONSIDER

How do clothes protect us?

What does a firefighter wear?

What does a ballerina wear?

What does an astronaut wear?

How do clothes help people do their jobs?

What clothing do we feel is appropriate for people in our family to wear?

START THE CONVERSATION

Explain to your child the many positive ways you can show affection: hugs, kisses, backrubs, holding hands, etc. Discuss the appropriate ways your family shows physical affection. Take the time to learn how your child feels affection: Touch? Words? Time? Service?

ADDITIONAL QUESTIONS TO CONSIDER

What are some ways that our family shows affection?

Do you like hugs?

Do you like to hear "I love you"?

Do you like to spend time together?

Do you like to sit on someone's lap?

Do you like talking?

Do you like playing together?

Out of all the ways our family shows affection, which ones are your favorites?

9.
GOOD TOUCH

- ONE WAY WE SHOW PEOPLE WE CARE ABOUT THEM IS THROUGH TOUCH

- WHAT KIND OF TOUCH DO YOU LIKE BEST? HUGS? KISSES? HIGH FIVES? KNUCKLES?

- CAN YOU THINK OF WAYS THAT OTHER PEOPLE OR EVEN ANIMALS EXPRESS AFFECTION TO EACH OTHER?

10. BAD TOUCH

- WE DO NOT ALLOW PEOPLE TO TOUCH US WHERE OUR UNDERWEAR COVERS

- PARENTS HELP US WASH OUR BODIES

- DOCTORS CAN EXAMINE YOU WHEN A PARENT IS THERE

- WHAT SHOULD YOU DO IF SOMEONE TOUCHES YOU IN A WAY THAT MAKES YOU FEEL UNCOMFORTABLE?

START THE CONVERSATION

Children may think that they will be punished if they tell an adult about a "bad" experience that happened to them simply because they were there during the experience. Help your child to understand that they are not in trouble if someone touches them where their underwear covers or in a way that makes them feel uncomfortable or confused. Reinforce that you will believe your child if they come to you with this information.

It may be helpful to practice ways that a child could approach a parent or trusted adult with information about "bad touching."

ADDITIONAL QUESTIONS TO CONSIDER

Is it ok for a _____ [teacher, coach, babysitter, etc.] to stroke your hair?

What kind of hug is ok?

Can bad touch happen when you have clothes on?

SAMPLE DIALOGUE

Parent: What should you do if someone touches you in a way that makes you feel uncomfortable?

Child: I don't know.

Parent: If anyone touches you where your underwear covers or in a way that makes you feel uncomfortable or confused, tell a parent or a trusted adult.

Child: Mom, someone helped me go to the bathroom and it made me uncomfortable.

Parent: Tell me what happened. You are safe and loved.

Child: Dad, someone helped me tuck in my shirt and I didn't like it.

Parent: Thank you for telling me. Let's talk about what happened so I can understand it better and help you.

SURVEY 1 **3-7**

Please reflect on your discussions with your child up to this point and answer the following questions.

1. Select the topic that has provided the best discussion with your child thus far.

    1. Amazing Bodies
    2. My Body Belongs to Me
    3. Male Anatomy
    4. Female Anatomy
    5. Respecting Others
    6. Public
    7. Private
    8. Clothing
    9. Good Touch
    10. Bad Touch

2. Referring to question 1, please describe what made this your best discussion.

    _____

    _____

3. Referring to question 1, were there things that you did during your discussion that were different from other discussions? If so, what were they and can you replicate them?

    _____

    _____

4. What has your child said that surprised you during your first 10 discussions?

_____

_____

5. If you have any additional comments, please write them here:

_____

_____

If you scan the code below, you can take this survey online. This will help us improve our curriculum and create new resources for parents.

11.
PREDATORS

- MOST PEOPLE ARE GOOD

- THESE ARE BAD PEOPLE:

- THESE ARE THE PEOPLE
  WE TRUST:

START THE CONVERSATION

It is important for every family to discuss who is a trusted non-family member. If there are known issues with any adults with whom your child has contact (including family members), create an appropriate plan with your child to deal with the situation. This may include things like not being alone with the person, not going places (especially alone) with the person, staying in the living room or yard and not going into a bedroom with the person, etc. Avoid blanket definitions (such as "We trust our teachers") because, unfortunately, that is not always true. Also explain that just because you "know" someone does not automatically mean that they are a trusted adult. Be specific and concrete in your planning in order to reassure and empower your child.

If your child is on the older end of this age spectrum, they can understand that some people might try to trick them or lie to them. Help them to see why this can be dangerous behavior and talk about ways they can avoid being tricked. Consider employing a "safe word" (a secret word that you agree on as a family) that you can give to other adults to let your child know that it is ok to do what that adult says (for example, if another adult needs to pick them up from school in the case of an emergency).

ADDITIONAL QUESTIONS TO CONSIDER

Who are some adults we trust?

Do you ever get an "icky" feeling around _____?

What can you do if an adult makes you uncomfortable?

Who is someone at school/church/soccer/etc. that you can talk to if a parent is not there?

START THE CONVERSATION

Discuss scenarios in which your child should say no, such as an adult helping a three-year-old in the bathroom may be appropriate, but in most circumstances, helping a seven-year-old is not. Practice these scenarios with your child.

Learning to say "No!" to an adult may not seem like a skill that you want to teach your child. However, consider the following: would you rather have to deal as a parent with a child that sometimes tells you no when you ask them to clean their room, or a child who is too uncomfortable or afraid to tell another adult no?

Help your child to understand when it's ok to say no to an adult by giving them specific examples.

Ok to say no:
When someone asks to see your private parts.

Not ok to say no:
When your parent tells you to pick up your toys.

12.
HOW TO SAY "NO"

- 🗨 YOU CAN SAY NO TO ANYONE

- 👑 WHEN IS IT OK TO SAY "NO"?

- 🗨 PRACTICE SAYING AND YELLING, "NO!"

13.
YOU HAVE INSTINCTS THAT KEEP YOU SAFE

- WHAT ARE INSTINCTS?

- WHAT DO INSTINCTS FEEL LIKE?

- WHAT DOES THAT "ICKY" FEELING MEAN?

- HAVE YOU EVER HAD THAT "ICKY" OR "SCARY" FEELING?

START THE CONVERSATION

As you practice, keep in mind the need to allow for your child's individual levels of maturity and development.

In order to explain the term "instinct" to your child, consider using the following simplified definition: something you know without learning it or thinking about it.

To help your child understand the role instincts can play, consider asking them how they feel when they:

- See an animal or insect they are afraid of

- See their favorite food

Explain to them that some instincts can keep us safe by warning us that something might be dangerous. Empower your child by helping them to recognize helpful instinctive responses.

CAUTION

Be careful not to introduce or reinforce fears. The goal of this conversation is not to create fear, but rather to help your child recognize negative responses they may have to potential molestation or other predatory behavior.

INSTINCTS: *An inherent inclination toward a particular behavior. Behavior that is performed without being based on prior experience is instinctive.*

START THE CONVERSATION

Explain to your child that there are different kinds of feelings between friends and within families. Talk about how it feels to be connected to other people. The point of this topic is to focus on the good and positive things that come out of family relationships. The healthy interactions that show love and concern should be stressed here.

ADDITIONAL QUESTIONS TO CONSIDER

What are the things that make our family special?

Why do we like to be with each other?

Why do we like to get together with family for the holidays, reunions, religious events, etc.?

14. YOU HAVE FEELINGS AND EMOTIONS THAT CONNECT YOU

- HOW DO YOU KNOW YOUR FAMILY LOVES YOU?

- THINK ABOUT YOUR FRIENDS: HOW DO YOU KNOW THEY LIKE YOU?

- TELL ME ABOUT THESE HAPPY FEELINGS

15.
ROMANTIC LOVE

- ⪜ WHAT IS ROMANTIC LOVE?

- ⪜ HOW IS IT DIFFERENT FROM OTHER KINDS OF LOVE?

- ⪜ HOW DO PEOPLE SHOW ROMANTIC LOVE?

START THE CONVERSATION
Take this opportunity to discuss and define romantic love as appropriate for your family. You may address the fact that it is something they will feel when they are older. Describe how you felt when you first fell in love.

ADDITIONAL QUESTIONS TO CONSIDER
What does it mean to fall in love?

Why is love so important?

START THE CONVERSATION

Talk about how children have lots of adults in their lives who take care of them in different ways. Explain that children need adults to help them learn and do things they can't do for themselves yet. They also need adults who care about them, not just for them.

ADDITIONAL QUESTIONS TO CONSIDER

How does your parent care for you?

How does your teacher care for you?

How does your grandparent care for you?

How does your _____ care for you? (someone other than these that your child may have.)

Explain that children need adults to help them learn and do things they can't do for themselves yet. They also need adults who care about them, not just for them.

16.
ADULTS WHO CARE FOR YOU

- THERE ARE MANY ADULTS WHO CARE FOR YOU

- THEY CARE FOR YOU IN DIFFERENT WAYS

- HOW DOES YOUR PARENT CARE FOR YOU?

17.
WHERE DO BABIES COME FROM?

- A BABY GROWS INSIDE A WOMAN'S UTERUS

- (IF READY) DESCRIBE HOW SPERM AND EGG CONNECT

- (IF READY) DESCRIBE BIRTH

- (IF READY) DEFINE THE WORD "SEX"

START THE CONVERSATION

Use your best judgment as to what level of information your child needs and/or is ready for. You know your child, so you know what they're ready to hear. Use their own terminology, but if you'd like them to use other words, now would be a good time to introduce terms that you prefer as a parent. Let your own understanding and love for your child determine the detail and depth of your discussion.

Many children know that women give birth to babies. If your child has questions concerning conception, gestation, and/or birth, answer them clearly and calmly, using correct terminology as applicable. Be sure to understand what the child's actual question is in order to avoid giving him or her answers that overwhelm them with unnecessary details and vocabulary.

ADDITIONAL QUESTIONS TO CONSIDER

Where did you come from?

Where do you think babies come from?

SAMPLE DIALOGUE

Child: Where do the mommies grow their babies?

Parent: Mommies have a special place in their tummies. It is called a "uterus." Babies grow inside the uterus until they are ready to be born.

Notice how the parent answers the question simply, defines terminology, and does not get distracted by additional details such as intercourse or birth.

START THE CONVERSATION

This discussion is a great opportunity to hear what your child thinks about who they might be when they grow up. Children often imagine a wide variety of careers or jobs for their future selves, but may not always take the time to conceptualize the ways their bodies will change as they mature.

SAMPLE ACTIVITY

Help your child visualize the changes their bodies will go through as they mature through a simple coloring activity.

On a sheet of paper, draw three basic people-shaped outlines. Make the first one small, the second one medium, and the third one tall. Then, ask your child to help draw or color (depending on their ability) themselves as an infant, a child, and an adult.

As you work together, ask them about their work and the choices they make. For example, "I see you've drawn a skirt on your grown up—are you going to wear skirts when you are a grown up? Why do you think you will do that?"

ADDITIONAL QUESTIONS TO CONSIDER

How tall do you think you will be when you are a grownup?

How will you wear your hair when you are older?

What do you think your body will look like when you are a grownup?

What parts of growing up are you excited about?

Are there any parts of growing up that make you nervous, or that you are worried about?

18.
WE CHANGE AND DEVELOP

- WE GROW TALLER AS WE GET OLDER

- WHAT ARE SOME OTHER CHANGES THAT HAPPEN TO YOU?

- HOW DO BOYS AND GIRLS LOOK DIFFERENT AS THEY GET OLDER?

19.
OTHER WORDS YOU'VE HEARD

- WHAT ARE SOME OTHER WORDS FOR PENIS?

- WHAT ARE SOME OTHER WORDS FOR VAGINA?

- WHAT ARE SOME OTHER WORDS FOR BREASTS?

START THE CONVERSATION

Depending on the age and past experiences of your child, it is possible that they will not necessarily have heard other words for one or more of these body parts. It is also possible that they will have heard many words for one or more of these body parts, and that they will find these words embarrassing or very funny. Decide beforehand how your family wants to refer to these body parts and help your child understand which terms are appropriate and which terms are inappropriate.

SAMPLE DIALOGUE

Child: I've heard breasts called boobies, titties, and hooties. (Giggles)

Parent: Some of those words sound pretty funny, don't they? But in our family, we are going to call them "breasts." Let's practice that word!

Child &
Parent: Breasts. Breasts! Breasts!
(Likely more giggling)

Parent: Wow! You can say "breasts" really well! That is the word we use in our family.

START THE CONVERSATION

As a parent, you will need to determine what levels of exploration are appropriate in your family. Children are naturally curious, and it is both normal and healthy for children to explore their bodies in a variety of ways. You may wish to provide some ground rules, such as "We don't touch our private parts around other people" or "We can talk about our bodies with our parents, but not with our teachers." Adapt any ground rules to fit the actual needs and concerns of your family and your child.

ADDITIONAL QUESTIONS TO CONSIDER

What are some amazing things our bodies do?

What do we do to take care of our bodies?

Additionally, this discussion can provide an excellent transition into a more detailed discussion about how our bodies work. Consider purchasing or checking out from the library a children's anatomy book to read with your child as part of or as a followup to this discussion.

20.
DISCOVERING OUR OWN BODIES

- ARE YOU CURIOUS ABOUT YOUR BODY?

- HOW CAN YOU GET TO KNOW YOUR BODY?

- DO YOU HAVE ANY QUESTIONS ABOUT YOUR BODY?

SURVEY 2 **3-7**

Please reflect on your discussions with your child up to this point and answer the following questions.

1. Select the topic that has been the most difficult to discuss with your child.

   11. Predators
   12. How to Say "No"
   13. You Have Instincts that Keep You Safe
   14. You Have Feelings and Emotions that Connect You
   15. Romantic Love
   16. Adults Who Care for You
   17. Where do Babies Come From?
   18. We Change and Develop
   19. Other Words You've Heard
   20. Discovering our Own Bodies

2. Referring to question 1, why was this topic difficult to discuss?

   _____

   _____

3. What have you said that has surprised you or exceeded your expectations of yourself in some way during the recent discussions?

   _____

   _____

4. What have you learned about your child during the recent discussions?

   _____

   _____

If you scan the code below, you can take this survey online. This will help us improve our curriculum and create new resources for parents.

21.
AFFECTION

- 👑 HOW DO WE SHOW AFFECTION TO OUR FRIENDS?

- 👑 WHAT IS THE DIFFERENCE BETWEEN PLAYING AND HITTING SOMEONE?

- 💬 SOMETIMES PLAYING CROSSES A LINE AND STOPS BEING FUN

- 👑 IS IT OKAY TO SAY "STOP" IF IT'S NOT FUN ANYMORE?

START THE CONVERSATION

The focus of this discussion is on peer relationships. Navigating peer relationships is a separate skill from that of adult-child interactions. It is important that your child learn both how to stop themselves from continuing behavior that has ceased to be fun for their friends as well as how to ask someone else to stop such behavior. Consider having your child practice the following in order to prepare them to say "stop" clearly and confidently, even when they are in a physically challenging situation.

ADDITIONAL QUESTIONS TO CONSIDER

How do you feel when _____ (a friend) gives you a high five?

How do you feel when _____ (a friend) shares a toy with you?

How do you feel when _____ (a friend) gives you a hug?

SAMPLE DIALOGUE

(for your child to practice)

Child: Please STOP tickling me; it is not fun anymore.
Child: You may not hit me. STOP hitting me.
Child: I do not want to wrestle anymore. Let's STOP.

Additionally, children should learn to show affection in good and appropriate ways. Help your child to understand that affection can be positive and help people to feel good about themselves when it is appropriately shared.

START THE CONVERSATION

When you have a friend, how can you be nice to them?
There are no right or wrong answers in this discussion. The point behind this discussion is to start thinking about gender roles. From a very early age, children learn to read social coding regarding what is appropriate for girls and what is appropriate for boys in terms of clothing, personal appearance, toys, colors, etc.

Empower your child by teaching them that gender does not need to determine or dictate the toys they play with. As an accompanying activity, consider holding a playtime with your child in which you deliberately introduce toys commonly associated with the opposite gender.

22.
PLAY

- DO YOU THINK THERE ARE DIFFERENT TOYS FOR BOYS AND GIRLS? WHY?

- DO YOU THINK THERE SHOULD BE "TOYS FOR BOYS" AND "TOYS FOR GIRLS"?

- HAVE YOU EVER FELT LIKE THERE WAS A TOY YOU COULDN'T PLAY WITH?

23.
HOW ARE BOYS AND GIRLS ALIKE?

- WE ALL START OUT AS BABIES

- WE ALL WANT TO BE LOVED AND HAVE FRIENDS

- WHAT ARE OTHER WAYS BOYS AND GIRLS CAN BE ALIKE?

START THE CONVERSATION

In discussing ways that boys and girls can be alike, consider the following examples:

> Hair and eye color can change from person to person. But, hair and eye color can also be the same for both a boy and a girl.

> Girls and boys both urinate. But girls sit down to urinate, and boys stand up.

After considering physical similarities, shift the conversation to emotions. Both boys and girls can, for example, be happy, feel sad, be scared, laugh, cry, etc. Emphasize the point that everyone, both boys and girls, has feelings and emotions.

ADDITIONAL QUESTIONS TO CONSIDER

Why are there boys and girls in the world?

What do boys contribute to the world?

What do girls contribute to the world?

24.
FRIENDSHIPS

- WHO ARE YOUR BEST FRIENDS?

- WHAT MAKES THEM GOOD FRIENDS?

- AS YOU GROW UP, FRIENDSHIPS CAN CHANGE

- IS IT POSSIBLE FOR BOYS AND GIRLS TO BE FRIENDS?

START THE CONVERSATION

As appropriate per your child's understanding and interest, this discussion can be continued as a discussion of how those friendships can change due to romantic feelings. Again, remind your child that they can always form appropriate friendships with both boys and girls. Teach your child that if they don't want to be friends with someone, they can (and must) at least respect each other.

ADDITIONAL QUESTIONS TO CONSIDER

What is respect?

How do we respect someone if we don't want to be their friend?

Who are the girls that you are friends with?

Who are the boys that you are friends with?

START THE CONVERSATION

Children may require assistance in the bathroom, even after they have been potty trained. Discuss appropriate ways to ask for help, when they should ask for help, and whom they should ask for help. Be as specific as possible in order to help your child be clear on both who and how they can ask for help. Adapt as appropriate to your child's specific situation and needs: preschool, play dates, church, with a babysitter, at a relative's house, etc.

ADDITIONAL DISCUSSION

Accidents happen. Bedwetting is common among young children, even after they have been toilet trained. Nighttime bladder control often is not achieved until the age of 6 or 7. However, children can be understandably sensitive regarding bedwetting, even to the point of trying to hide the accident. The purpose of the following discussion points is to both reassure your child that they will not be in trouble if they do have an accident, and to help both you and your child develop a plan for what to do if an accident does occur.

- Sometimes, we may wet the bed at night
- Sometimes, we may wet our clothing
- If you have an accident, who should you ask for help?

SAMPLE DIALOGUE

(for child to practice)

Child: I need help wiping after I poop.
Aunt Cindy, can you help me?

Child: I need help pulling up my pants.
Dad, can you help me?

25.
MY BODY POOPS AND PEES

- 💬 **EVERYBODY HAS BOWEL MOVEMENTS**

- 💬 **EVERYBODY URINATES**

- 👑 **IF YOU NEED HELP WHILE GOING TO THE BATHROOM, WHAT SHOULD YOU DO?**

- 💬 **ACCIDENTS CAN HAPPEN**

26.
PORNOGRAPHY

- PORNOGRAPHY IS PICTURES OR MOVIES OF PEOPLE WITH LITTLE OR NO CLOTHES ON

- (IF APPROPRIATE TO SHARE) THEY SHOW PRIVATE ACTIONS TO MAKE MONEY

- NO ONE SHOULD MAKE YOU LOOK AT PICTURES OR MOVIES THAT MAKE YOU FEEL UNCOMFORTABLE

- WHAT WOULD YOU DO IF YOU SAW A PICTURE THAT MADE YOU FEEL UNCOMFORTABLE?

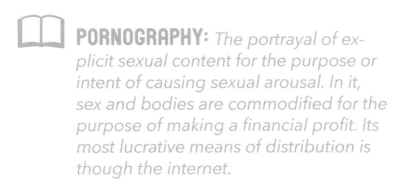

PORNOGRAPHY: *The portrayal of explicit sexual content for the purpose or intent of causing sexual arousal. In it, sex and bodies are commodified for the purpose of making a financial profit. Its most lucrative means of distribution is though the internet.*

START THE CONVERSATION

Because pornography is a prevalent part of modern popular culture, children are exposed to it at younger and younger ages. Children's brains are not equipped to deal with the images of pornography. As a parent, you will need to determine when and where your child may be exposed to pornography and how to prevent such exposure. Ensure that appropriate filters are in place on all internet-enabled devices, and that all adult media content is appropriately contained both in their own home and in homes that they regularly visit.

At this young age, it is especially important that children develop a healthy sense of their own bodily integrity. As such, arbitrary rules regarding nudity such as "It is always bad to be naked" can cause unintentional damage by promoting an underlying sense of shame and even loathing with regards to the body. Determine as a family what the appropriate boundaries regarding nudity are for your personal situation, and avoid associating shame with bodies.

ASK YOUR CHILD
Have you ever seen pictures or movies of naked people?

WHAT TO DO IF YOUR CHILD HAS BEEN EXPOSED TO PORNOGRAPHY
Despite one's best efforts, during this discussion it may become clear that your child has been exposed to pornography. If this is the case,

1) Don't overreact or shame your child.

2) Determine the severity and nature of what was seen. More sexually explicit or violent material may be traumatic for young children.

3) Ask your child:
   How did it make you feel when you saw it?
4) Take apart what they saw—help your child to understand that such images are altered and that they do not reflect reality.

If your child is traumatized, starts to actively seek out por- nographic content, or starts to imitate explicit sexual acts either alone or with other children, professional help may be needed.

"AT THIS YOUNG AGE, IT IS ESPECIALLY IMPORTANT THAT CHILDREN DEVELOP A HEALTHY SENSE OF THEIR OWN BODILY INTEGRITY."

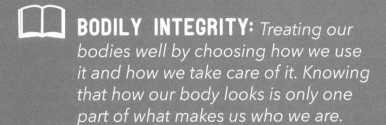

BODILY INTEGRITY: *Treating our bodies well by choosing how we use it and how we take care of it. Knowing that how our body looks is only one part of what makes us who we are.*

27.
PICTURES

- HOW MANY WAYS CAN YOU THINK OF TO TAKE PICTURES IN YOUR HOUSE?

- PEOPLE TAKE PICTURES ALL THE TIME ON THEIR PHONES

- WHEN IS IT OKAY TO TAKE A PICTURE OF SOMEONE?

- WHEN IS IT OKAY TO HAVE SOMEONE TAKE A PICTURE OF YOU?

START THE CONVERSATION

As a parent, you have a responsibility to help protect your child from potential dangers that they do not yet comprehend. The ease and prevalence with which we as a society produce pictures can give a child the impression that all pictures are good, fun, happy things. They do not comprehend the rapid way in which an inappropriate photograph may be disseminated via text messaging and the internet to a large, public audience. Determine what limitations, if any, you wish to place on picture taking and picture sharing, and explain them clearly to your child.

SAMPLE SCENARIO

Before beginning this activity, contact another trusted adult (spouse, grandparent, etc.) and arrange a time to call them on the phone as part of this activity.

Give your child a camera, phone, or other device capable of taking pictures and let them take a few. If possible, take a few selfies with yourself and your child. Explain to them that pictures can be a fun way to express affection and closeness.

Next, text or email a photo of your child to the trusted adult you contacted earlier. Have the adult call the child on the phone and describe to them the picture that the child just sent them. Help the child see that sending pictures can happen quickly, and that other people can see the pictures they send. Reinforce the limitations your family has placed on taking and sharing pictures.

To help your child understand that this happens with both good and bad pictures, ask them: What kinds of pictures are not ok to send? What makes certain pictures "not ok" to send?

START THE CONVERSATION

Every family will have different rules regarding the use of electronic devices. Make sure that your child clearly understands what your family rules are and how they will be enforced. Children will often share electronic devices in order to share games or "take turns." Be up front with other parents regarding your family's policies. Ask other parents what their preferences are with regards to electronic content and devices. Even if another parent has not thought through these issues, by asking them about it you raise awareness and promote a culture of responsible media consumption.

Help your child understand that they should take the electronic device directly to a trusted adult if it begins to display images that make them uncomfortable. Be sure to reinforce this behavior in your children by praising them when they do bring something to you to show you—resist the temptation to get upset if they bring you something trivial or inconsequential. The important pattern to develop here is a pattern of trust: you want your child to trust you and turn to you when they encounter things that they don't understand or that are unsettling to them, so that, if they ever should encounter something potentially harmful or dangerous, they will turn to you rather than hide.

ADDITIONAL QUESTIONS TO CONSIDER

In our house, when can we watch TV?

In our house, when can we play on the computer/iPod/phone/tablet/etc.?

What movies are ok for us to watch at our house?
At a friend's house?

28.
COMPUTERS
& THE
INTERNET

- WHAT IS YOUR FAVORITE GAME TO PLAY ON A COMPUTER, DEVICES, ETC?

- WHAT SHOULD YOU DO IF YOUR ELECTRONIC DEVICE SHOWS YOU PICTURES THAT MAKE YOU UNCOMFORTABLE?

- WHAT DO WE DO IF OUR FRIENDS OFFER TO LET US USE THEIR DEVICES?

29.
NUDITY

- NUDE/NUDITY/NAKED

- IS NUDITY OKAY IN OUR HOUSE?

- WHAT DO WE DO IF WE ACCIDENTALLY SEE SOMEONE NAKED?

START THE CONVERSATION

Children often consider nudity to be funny; it is common for young children to incorporate nudity into their imaginative play. Determine what your family rules regarding nudity are, and help your child understand the limitations you place on nudity.

SAMPLE DIALOGUE

Parent: Sarah, please close the bathroom door.
I am taking a shower and would like my privacy.
Child: I see your bum! Ha ha ha ha!
Parent: Sarah, in our family we do not laugh and point
at people who are taking a shower.
You need to apologize.

START THE CONVERSATION

Take this opportunity to reinforce your child's sense of self-worth and their own belief in their individual beauty. At this age, children often associate beauty with external qualities. Help them to understand that beauty and strength are internal qualities. For example, you may wish to have them think of someone they love and admire, such as a grandparent, teacher, or friend. Point out the ways that that person is beautiful through the actions they take, the words they say, or the way they make your child feel loved and accepted. Ask your child: What are some things or people that you consider beautiful?

ADDITIONAL QUESTIONS TO CONSIDER

Why do we like beautiful things?

What are your favorite things about your body?

What makes you special?

30.
I AM BEAUTIFUL AND STRONG

- ♛ WHAT MAKES SOMETHING BEAUTIFUL?

- ♛ WHAT MAKES SOMETHING STRONG?

- ♛ CAN A PERSON'S "INSIDES" BE BEAUTIFUL?

- ♛ HOW DO YOU SHOW PEOPLE THAT YOU ARE BEAUTIFUL AND STRONG?

SURVEY 3 **3-7**

Thank you for using 30 Days of Sex Talks. Please answer the following questions to help us continue to improve our program.

1. Did you use the sample dialogues and/or activities during your discussions?

   Yes   No

2. Referring to question 1, which dialogues and/or activities worked best and worst for your child?

   Best_____
   Worst_____

3. Please select the topic (if any) that was the most difficult to discuss.

   1. Amazing Bodies
   2. My Body Belongs to Me
   3. Male Anatomy
   4. Female Anatomy
   5. Respecting Others
   6. Public
   7. Private
   8. Clothing
   9. Good Touch
   10. Bad Touch
   11. Predators
   12. How to Say "No"
   13. You Have Instincts that Keep You Safe
   14. You Have Feelings and Emotions that Connect You
   15. Romantic Love
   16. Adults Who Care for You
   17. Where do Babies Come From?

18. We Change and Develop
19. Other Words You've Heard
20. Discovering our Own Bodies
21. Affection
22. Play
23. How are Boys and Girls Alike?
24. Friendships
25. My Body Poops and Pees!
26. Pornography
27. Pictures
28. Computers and the Internet
29. Nudity
30. I Am Beautiful and Strong

4. Referring to question 3, why was this topic difficult to discuss?

_____

_____

5. Having completed this program, please rate your current comfort level of discussing human sexuality with your child.

1   2   3   4   5   6   7   8   9   10

Low   Medium   High

6. Do you feel that your ability to discuss difficult things with your child has been enhanced by these discussions? Please explain your answer.

Yes   No

_____

_____

7. Was there anything that you learned from your child that surprised you (good or bad)? Please describe below.

_____

_____

8. Do you feel that this experience has increased the likelihood of your child coming to you with questions about sex and sexuality?

Yes   No

9. Rate the effectiveness of the overall program below.

1   2   3   4   5   6   7   8   9   10

Low   Medium   High

10. Would you recommend this program to your friends and family?

Yes   No

11. Is there anything that you think the program needs to improve, add, or remove? If so, please explain.

If you scan the code below, you can take this survey online. This will help us improve our curriculum and create new resources for parents.

FREE DOWNLOADABLE!

This curriculum works best when it is interactive between you and your child. To help facilitate this interaction, we've developed topic cards as a companion to this book. The topic cards are a bonus for you to download at your convenience. They can be printed and placed on the refrigerator, on a mirror, in your pocket or wherever they need to be to serve as a reminder to both you and your child to **start talking!**

To obtain your free download, please scan the QR code below and enter the following password: 3edcVFR$

IF YOU ENJOYED THIS BOOK, PLEASE LEAVE A POSITIVE REVIEW ON AMAZON.COM

For great resources and information, follow us on our social media outlets:

Facebook: www.facebook.com/educateempowerkids/
Twitter: @EduEmpowerKids
Pinterest: pinterest.com/educateempower/
Instagram: Eduempowerkids

Subscribe to our website for exclusive offers and information at: www.educateempowerkids.org

REFERENCES AND RESOURCES

Strengthening your child
30 Days to a Stronger Child, http://amzn.to/25t8l0J

Talking to kids about pornography
How to Talk to Your Kids About Pornography, http://amzn.to/ß1OjQKfA

Hilton, D., & Watts, C. (2011, February 21). Pornography addiction: A neuroscience perspective. Retrieved from http://www.ncbi.nlm.nih.gov/pmc/articles/PMC3050060/

Layden, M. (n.d.). Pornography and Violence: A New Look at Research. Retrieved from http://www.socialcostsofpornography.com/Layden_Pornography_and_Violence.pdf

Voon, V. et. al. (2014, July 11). Neural Correlates of Sexual Cue Reactivity in Individuals with and without Compulsive Sexual Behaviours. Retrieved from http://www.plosone.org/article/info%3Adoi%2F10.1371%2Fjournal.pone.0102419

Rape culture resource
http://www.marshall.edu/wcenter/sexual-assault/rape-culture/

Predator-victim grooming resource
http://www.parenting.org/article/victim-grooming-protect-your-child-from-sexual-predators

Slut-shaming study
http://america.aljazeera.com/articles/2014/5/29/slut-shaming-study.html

Birth control resource
http://www.mayoclinic.org/healthy-living/birth-control/basics/birth-control-basics/hlv-20049454

Pregnancy rates
http://www.hhs.gov/ash/oah/adolescent-health-topics/reproductive-health/teen-pregnancy/trends.html#.VBy66hB0ypo

Pregnancy resource
http://www.whattoexpect.com/what-to-expect/landing-page.
aspx

STD/STI resource
http://www.womenshealth.gov/publications/our-publications/
fact-sheet/sexually-transmitted-infections.html

STD/STI rates
http://www.cdc.gov/std/stats/STI-Estimates-Fact-Sheet-
Feb-2013.pdf

Domestic violence resource
http://www.justice.gov/ovw/domestic-violence

Domestic violence resource
http://www.thehotline.org/

Information on masturbation and porn use
http://blogs.psychcentral.com/sex/2011/04/compulsive-mastur-
bation-and-porn/

Creating a family media standard
http://bit.ly/1xwb1ri

Lesson on Media Literacy
http://bit.ly/1iZifnh

Videos related to the 30 Days of Sex Talks books
http://bit.ly/29zyVNW

GLOSSARY

The following terms have been included to assist you as you prepare and hold discussions with your children regarding healthy sexuality and intimacy. The definitions are not intended for the child; rather, they are meant to clarify the concepts and terms for the adult. Some terms may not be appropriate for your child, given their age, circumstances, or your own family culture and values. Use your judgment to determine which terminology best meets your individual needs.

Abstinence: The practice of not doing or having something that is wanted or enjoyable: the practice of abstaining from something.

Abuse: The improper usage or treatment of another person or entity, often to unfairly gain power or other benefit in the relationship.

Affection: A feeling or type of love that exceeds general goodwill.

AIDS: A sexually transmitted or bloodborne viral infection that causes immune deficiency.

Anal Sex: A form of intercourse that generally involves the insertion and thrusting of the erect penis into the anus or rectum for sexual pleasure.

Anus: The external opening of the rectum comprised of two sphincters which control the exit of feces from the body.

Appropriate: Suitable, proper, or fitting for a particular purpose, person, or circumstance.

Arousal: The physical and emotional response to sexual desire during or in anticipation of sexual activity.

Bisexual: Sexual orientation in which one is attracted to both males and females.

Body Image: An individual's feelings regarding their own physical attractiveness and sexuality. These feelings and opinions are often influenced by other people and media sources.

Bodily Integrity: The personal belief that our bodies, while crucial to our understanding of who we are, do not in themselves solely define our worth; the knowledge that our bodies are the storehouse of our humanity; and the sense that we esteem our bodies and we treat them accordingly.

Boundaries: The personal limits or guidelines that an individual forms in order to clearly identify what are reasonable and safe behaviors for others to engage in around him or her.

Bowel Movement: Also known as defecation, a bowel movement is the final act of digestion by which waste is eliminated from the body via the anus.

Breasts: Women develop breasts on their upper torso during puberty. Breasts contain mammary glands, which create the breast milk used to feed infants.

Child: A person between birth and full growth.

Chlamydia: Bacteria that causes or is associated with various diseases of the eye and urogenital tract.

Clitoris: A female sex organ visible at the front juncture of the labia minora above the opening of the urethra. The clitoris is the female's most sensitive erogenous zone.

Condom: A thin rubber covering that a man wears on his penis during sex in order to prevent a woman from becoming pregnant or to prevent the spread of diseases.

Consent: Clear agreement or permission to permit something or to do something. Consent must be given freely, without force or intimidation, and while the person is fully conscious and cognizant of their present situation.

Contraceptive: A method, device, or medication that works to prevent pregnancy. Another name for birth control.

Curiosity: The desire to learn or know more about something or someone.

Date Rape: A rape in which the perpetrator has a relationship that is, to some degree, either romantic or potentially sexual with the victim. The perpetrator uses physical force, psychological intimidation, or drugs or alcohol to force the victim to have sex either against their will or in a state in which they cannot give clear consent.

Degrade: To treat with contempt or disrespect.

Demean: To cause a severe loss in the dignity of or respect for another person.

Derogatory: An adjective that implies severe criticism or loss of respect.

Diaphragm: A cervical barrier type of birth control made of a soft latex or silicone dome with a spring molded into the rim. The spring creates a seal against the walls of the vagina, preventing semen, including sperm, from entering the fallopian tubes.

Domestic Abuse/Domestic Violence: A pattern of abusive behavior in any relationship that is used by one partner to gain or maintain power and control over another intimate partner. It can be physical, sexual, emotional, economic, or psychological actions or threats of actions that influence another person. (DOJ definition)

Double Standard: A rule or standard that is applied differently and unfairly to a person or distinct groups of people.

Egg Cell: The female reproductive cell, which, when fertilized by sperm inside the uterus, will eventually grow into an infant.

Ejaculation: When a man reaches orgasm, during which semen is expelled from the penis.

Emotional Abuse: A form of abuse in which another person is subjected to behavior that can result in psychological trauma. Emotional abuse often occurs within relationships in which there is a power imbalance.

Emotional Intimacy: As aspect of relationships that is dependent upon trust and that can be expressed both verbally and non-verbally. Emotional intimacy displays a degree of closeness that exceeds that normally experienced in common relational interactions.

Epididymal Hypertension: A condition that results from prolonged sexual arousal in human males in which fluid congestion in the testicles occurs, often accompanied by testicular pain. The condition is temporary. Also referred to as "blue balls."

Erection: During a penile erection, the penis becomes engorged and enlarged due to the dilation of the cavernosal arteries (which run the length of the penis) and subsequent engorgement of the surrounding corporal tissue with blood.

Explicit: An adjective signifying that something is stated clearly, without room for confusion or doubt. Sexually explicit material, however, signifies that the content contains sexual material that may be considered offensive or overtly graphic.

Extortion: To obtain something through force or via threats.

Family: A group consisting of parents and children living together in a household. The definition of family is constantly evolving, and every person can define family in a different way to encompass the relationships he or she shares with people in his or her life. Over time one's family will change as one's life changes and the importance of family values and rituals deepen.

Female Arousal: The physiological responses to sexual desire during or in anticipation of sexual activity in women include vaginal lubrication (wetness), engorgement of the external genitals (clitoris and labia), enlargement of the vagina, and dilation of the pupils.

Fertilize: The successful union between an egg (technically known as the ovum) and a sperm, which normally occurs within the second portion of the fallopian tube (known as the ampulla). The result of fertilization is a zygote (fertilized egg).

Friend: Someone with whom a person has a relationship of mutual affection. A friend is closer than an associate or acquaintance. Friends typically share emotions and characteristics such as affection, empathy, honesty, trust, and compassion.

Gay: A word used to describe people who are sexually attracted to members of the same sex. The term "lesbian" is generally preferred when talking about women who are attracted to other women. Originally, the word "gay" meant "carefree"; its connection to sexual orientation developed during the latter half of the 20th century.

Gender: Masculinity and femininity are differentiated through a range of characteristics known as "gender." They may include biological sex (being male or female), social roles based upon biological sex, and one's subjective experience and understanding of their own gender identity.

Gender Role: The pattern of masculine or feminine behavior of an individual that is defined by a particular culture and that is largely determined by a child's upbringing.

Gender Stereotypes: A thought or understanding applied to either males or females (or other gender identities) that may or may not correspond with reality. "Men don't cry" or "women are weak" are examples of inaccurate gender stereotypes.

Gestation: The time when a person or animal is developing inside its mother before it is born.

Gonorrhea: A contagious inflammation of the genital mucous membrane caused by the gonococcus.

Groom: To prepare or train someone for a particular purpose or activity. In the case of sexual predators, it is any willful action made by the offender to prepare the victim and/or the victim's support network that allows for easier sex offending.

Healthy Sexuality: Having the ability to express one's sexuality in ways that contribute positively to one's own self-esteem and relationships. Healthy sexuality includes approaching sexual relationships and interactions with mutual agreement and dignity. It necessarily includes mutual respect and a lack of fear, shame, or guilt, and never includes coercion or violence.

Hepatitis B: A sometimes fatal disease caused by a double-stranded DNA virus that tends to persist in the blood serum and is transmitted especially by contact with infected blood (as by transfusion or by sharing contaminated needles in illicit intravenous drug use) or by contact with other infected bodily fluids such as semen.

Hepatitis C: Caused by a single-stranded RNA virus of the family Flaviviridae that tends to persist in the blood serum and is usually transmitted by infected blood (as by injection of an illicit drug, blood transfusion, or exposure to blood or blood products).

Herpes: Any of several inflammatory diseases of the skin caused by herpes viruses and characterized by clusters of vesicles.

Heterosexual: Sexual orientation in which one is attracted to members of the opposite sex (males are attracted to females; females are attracted to males).

HIV: Any of several retroviruses and especially HIV-1 that infect and destroy helper T cells of the immune system causing the marked reduction in their numbers that is diagnostic of AIDS.

Homosexual: Sexual orientation in which one is attracted to members of the same sex (males are attracted to males; females are attracted to females).

Hook up Sex: A form of casual sex in which sexual activity takes place outside the context of a committed relationship. The sex may be a one-time event, or an ongoing arrangement; in either case, the focus is generally on the physical enjoyment of sexual activity without an emotional involvement or commitment.

HPV: Human papillomavirus.

Hymen: A membrane that partially closes the opening of the vagina and whose presence is traditionally taken to be a mark of virginity. However, it can often be broken before a woman has sex simply by being active, and sometimes it is not present at all.

Hyper-sexualized: To make extremely sexual; to accentuate the sexuality of. Often seen in media.

Instinct: An inherent inclination towards a particular behavior. Behavior that is performed without being based on prior experience is instinctive.

Intercourse: Sexual activity, also known as coitus or copulation, which is most commonly understood to refer to the insertion of the penis into the vagina (vaginal sex). It should be noted that there are a wide range of various sexual activities and the boundaries of what constitutes sexual intercourse are still under debate.

Intimacy: Generally a feeling or form of significant closeness. There are four types of intimacy: physical intimacy (sensual proximity or touching), emotional intimacy (close connection resulting from trust and love), cognitive or intellectual intimacy (resulting from honest exchange of thoughts and ideas), and experiential intimacy (a connection that occurs while acting together). Emotional and physical intimacy are often associated with sexual relationships, while intellectual and experiential intimacy are not.

Labia: The inner and outer folds of the vulva on both sides of the vagina.

Lesbian: A word used to describe women who are sexually attracted to other women.

Lice (Pubic): A sucking louse infesting the pubic region of the human body.

Love: A wide range of emotional interpersonal connections, feelings, and attitudes. Common forms include kinship or familial love, friendship, divine love (as demonstrated through worship), and sexual or romantic love. In biological terms, love is the attraction and bonding that functions to unite human beings and facilitate the social and sexual continuation of the species.

Masturbation: The self-stimulation of the genitals in order to produce sexual arousal, pleasure, and orgasm.

Media Literacy: The various tools and competencies used to aid people in approaching media (including advertising, television, magazines, social media, and other media forms) critically. A critical approach to media focuses on analyzing and evaluating the media in terms of its intended audience, message, and creator, as well as noting the various ways in which facts are manipulated, spun, or even discarded in order to promote a particular reaction or interpretation.

Menstrual Cycle: Egg is released from ovaries through fallopian tube into uterus. Each month, blood and tissue build up in the uterus. When the egg is not fertilized, this blood and tissue are not needed and are shed from the body through the vagina. Cycle is roughly 28 days but can vary. Bleeding time lasts from 2-7 days. May be accompanied by cramping, breast tenderness, and emotional sensitivity.

Menstrual Period: A discharging of blood, secretions, and tissue debris from the uterus at periods of approximately one month in females of breeding age that are not pregnant.

Misogyny: The hatred, aversion, hostility, or dislike of women or girls. Misogyny can appear in a single individual, or may also be manifest in broad cultural trends that undermine women's autonomy and value.

Monogamy: A relationship in which a person has one partner at any one time.

Nipples: The circular, somewhat conical structure of tissue on the breast. The skin of the nipple and its surrounding areola are often several shades darker than that of the surrounding breast tissue. In women, the nipple delivers breast milk to infants.

Nocturnal Emissions   A spontaneous orgasm that occurs during sleep. Nocturnal emissions can occur in both males (ejaculation) and females (lubrication of the vagina). The term "wet dream" is often used to describe male nocturnal emissions.

Nudity: The state of not wearing any clothing. Full nudity denotes a complete absence of clothing, while partial nudity is a more ambiguous term, denoting the presence of an indeterminate amount of clothing.

Oral Sex: Sexual activity that involves stimulation of the genitals through the use of another person's mouth.

Orgasm: The rhythmic muscular contractions in the pelvic region that occur as a result of sexual stimulation, arousal, and activity during the sexual response cycle. Orgasms are characterized by a sudden release of built-up sexual tension and by the resulting sexual pleasure.

Penis: The external male sexual organ comprised of the shaft, foreskin, glans penis, and meatus. The penis contains the urethra, through which both urine and semen travel to exit the body.

Perception: A way of regarding, understanding, or interpreting something; a mental impression

Period: The beginning of the menstrual cycle.

Physical Abuse: The improper physical treatment of another person or entity designed to cause bodily harm, pain, injury, or other suffering. Physical abuse is often employed to unfairly gain power or other benefit in the relationship.

The Pill: An oral contraceptive for women containing the hormones estrogen and progesterone or progesterone alone, that inhibits ovulation, fertilization, or implantation of a fertilized ovum, causing temporary infertility. Common brands include Ortho Tri-Cyclen, Yasmin, and Ortho-Novum.

Pornography: The portrayal of explicit sexual content for the purpose or intent of causing sexual arousal. In it, sex and bodies are commodified for the purpose of making a financial profit. It can be created in a variety of media contexts, including videos, photos, animation, books and magazines. Its most lucrative means of distribution is though the internet. The industry that creates pornography is a sophisticated, corporatized, billion dollar business.

Positive Self-Talk: Anything said to oneself for encouragement or motivation, such as phrases or mantras; also, one's ongoing internal conversation with oneself, like a running commentary, which influences how one feels and behaves.

Predator: A predator is technically an organism or being that hunts and then feeds on their prey. A sexual predator is someone who seeks to obtain sexual contact through "hunting." The term is often used to describe the deceptive and coercive methods used by people who commit sex crimes where there is a victim, such as rape or child abuse.

Pregnancy: The common term used for gestation in humans. During pregnancy, the embryo or fetus grows and develops inside a woman's uterus.

Premature Ejaculation: When a man regularly reaches orgasm, during which semen is expelled from the penis, prior to or within one minute of the initiation of sexual activity.

Priapism: The technical term of a condition in which the erect penis does not return to flaccidity within four hours, despite the absence of physical or psychological sexual stimulation.

Private: Belonging to or for the use of a specific individual. Private and privacy denote a state of being alone, solitary, individual, exclusive, secret, personal, hidden, and confidential.

Psychological Abuse: A form of abuse in which a person is subjected to behavior that can result in psychological trauma. Psychological abuse often occurs within relationships in which there is a power imbalance.

Puberty: A period or process through which children reach sexual maturity. Once a person has reached puberty, their body is capable of sexual reproduction.

Public: Belonging to or for the use of all people in a specific area, or all people as a whole. Something that is public is common, shared, collective, communal, and widespread.

Rape: A sex crime in which the perpetrator forces another person to have sexual intercourse against their will and without consent. Rape often occurs through the threat or actuality of violence against the victim.

Rape Culture: A culture in which rape is pervasive and to an extent normalized due to cultural and societal attitudes towards gender and sexuality. Behaviors that facilitate rape culture include victim blaming, sexual objectification, and denial regarding sexual violence.

Relationship: The state of being connected with another person or the way in which two people are connected.

Rhythm Method: A method of avoiding pregnancy by restricting sexual intercourse to the times of a woman's menstrual cycle when ovulation and conception are least likely to occur. Because it can be difficult to predict ovulation and because abstinence has to be practiced for up to ten days of a woman's cycle, the effectiveness of the rhythm method is on average just 75-87%, according to http://www.webmd.com.

Romantic Love: A form of love that denotes intimacy and a strong desire for emotional connection with another person to whom one is generally also sexually attracted.

Scrotum: The pouch of skin underneath the penis that contains the testicles.

Self-Esteem / Self -Worth: An individual's overall emotional evaluation of their own worth. Self-esteem is both a judgment of the self and an attitude toward the self. More generally, the term is used to describe a confidence in one's own value or abilities.

Semen: The male reproductive fluid, which contains spermatozoa in suspension. Semen exits the penis through ejaculation.

Serial Monogamy: A mating system in which a man or woman can only form a long-term, committed relationship (such as marriage) with one partner at a time. Should the relationship dissolve, the individual may go on to form another relationship, but only after the first relationship has ceased.

Sexting: The sending or distribution of sexually explicit images, messages, or other material via mobile phones.

Sexual Abuse: The improper sexual usage or treatment of another person or entity, often to unfairly gain power or other benefit in the relationship. In instances of sexual abuse, undesired sexual behaviors are forced upon one person by another.

Sexual Assault: A term often used in legal contexts to refer to sexual violence. Sexual assault occurs when there is any non-consensual sexual contact or violence. Examples include rape, groping, forced kissing, child sexual abuse, and sexual torture.

Sexual Harassment: Harassment involving unwanted sexual advances or obscene remarks. Sexual harassment can be a form of sexual coercion as well as an undesired sexual proposition, including the promise of reward in exchange for sexual favors.

Sexual Identification: How one thinks of oneself in terms of whom one is romantically or sexually attracted to.

Sexual Molestation: Aggressive and persistent harassment, either psychological or physical, of a sexual manner.

Shame: The painful feeling arising from the consciousness of something dishonorable, improper, ridiculous, etc., done by oneself or another.

Slut-shaming: The act of criticizing, attacking, or shaming a woman for her real or presumed sexual activity, or for behaving in ways that someone thinks are associated with her real or presumed sexual activity.

Sperm: The male reproductive cell, consisting of a head, midpiece, and tail. The head contains the genetic material, while the tail is used to propel the sperm as it travels towards the egg.

Spontaneous Erection: A penile erection that occurs as an automatic response to a variety of stimuli, some of which is sexual and some of which is physiological.

STD: An abbreviation that refers to sexually transmitted diseases. These are illnesses that are communicable through sexual behaviors, including intercourse. Some of these illnesses can also be transmitted through blood contact.

STI: An abbreviation that refers to sexually transmitted infections. These are illnesses that are communicable through sexual behaviors, including intercourse. Some of these illnesses can also be transmitted through blood contact. Not all STI's lead to a disease and become an STD.

Straight: A slang term for heterosexuality, a sexual orientation in which one is attracted to members of the opposite sex (males are attracted to females; females are attracted to males).

Syphilis: A chronic, contagious, usually venereal and often congenital, disease caused by a spirochete, and if left untreated, producing chancres, rashes, and systemic lesions in a clinical course with three stages continued over many years.

Test Touch: Seemingly innocent touches by a predator or offender, such as a pat on the back or a squeeze on the arm, that are meant to normalize kids to being in physical contact with the predator. Test touches can progress to trying to be alone with the child.

Testicles: The male gonad, which is located inside the scrotum beneath the penis. The testicles are responsible for the production of sperm and androgens, primarily testosterone.

Transgender: A condition or state in which one's physical sex does not match one's gender identity. A transgender individual may have been assigned a sex at birth based on their genitals, but feel that this assignation is false or incomplete. They also may be someone who does not conform to conventional gender roles but instead combines or moves between them.

Uncomfortable: Feeling or causing discomfort or unease; disquieting.

Under the Influence: Being physically affected by alcohol or drugs

Urethra: The tube that connects the urinary bladder to the urinary meatus (the orifice through which the urine exits the urethra tube). In males, the urethra runs down the penis and opens at the end of the penis. In females, the urethra is internal and opens between the clitoris and the vagina.

Urination: The process through which urine is released from the urinary bladder to travel down the urethra and exit the body at the urinary meatus.

Uterus: A major reproductive sex organ in the female body. The uterus is located in the lower half of the torso, just above the vagina. It is the site in which offspring are conceived and in which they gestate during the term of the pregnancy.

Vagina: The muscular tube leading from the external genitals to the cervix of the uterus in women. During sexual intercourse, the penis can be inserted into the vagina. During childbirth, the infant exits the uterus through the vagina.

Vaginal Sex: A form of sexual intercourse in which the penis is inserted into the vagina.

Vaginismus: A medical condition in which a woman is unable to engage in any form of vaginal penetration, including sexual intercourse, the use of tampons or menstrual cups, and that of gynecological examinations, due to involuntary pain.

Victim: A person who is harmed, injured, or killed as the result of an accident or crime.

Virgin: A male or female who has never engaged in sexual intercourse.

Vulva: The parts of the female sexual organs that are on the outside of the body.

Wet Dreams : A slang term for nocturnal emissions. A nocturnal emission is a spontaneous orgasm that occurs during sleep. Nocturnal emissions can occur in both males (ejaculation) and females (lubrication of the vagina).

Printed in Great Britain
by Amazon